The Gift Birthed…
After My Loss

ELANA L. BURNES 2/22/2018

THANK YOU CINNAMON FOR YOUR
SUPPORT, MAY GOD GIVE THE DESIRES
OF YOUR HEART.

MUCH LOVE TO YOU.

Published by: D&E Productions

Edited by : Drenda Davis-Jackson

ISBN-10: 1982083174

ISBN-13: 9781982083175

THE GIFT BIRTHED...AFTER MY LOSS

DEDICATION

I would like to dedicate this book in the loving memory of my son,

Trazel D. Spencer

It is through the trial of his death that God birthed such an amazingly beautiful gift. Losing him pushed me out of a marriage of almost thirty years and a house I no longer wanted to be in. The loss of my son gave me the strength that I needed to be set free.

For a long time I couldn't even verbalize the fact that losing him set me free. It was painful just to think along those lines; however that was my reality. Trazel passed at the age of thirty-one on May 29,2011 Five months after his passing, on October 29, 2011, I realized life was too short to be miserable. I thank God for setting me free and bringing me back together.

ACKNOWLEDGEMENTS

I would first like to thank God for entrusting me with such a precious gift.

I would like to thank *Minister Nannette Conyers* for her obedience in delivering the message from God, and continuously supporting, encouraging, and praying for me.

I thank God for *Yvonne Brown*, and *Trellany Roberts* they have been on this journey with me from day one. They have not missed not one day of supporting me. Only God can choose someone to be as diligent as they have been.

I am thankful for *Ola Montaque* for her obedience in sending me pictures of the sunrise when the Holy Spirit led her to. She has also continued to support me.

I am so very grateful for *Pastor Betty Ferguson*, who God chose to give me instructions and pieces of the puzzle I needed in beginning the process in understanding and starting ministry.

And last but not least, I thank my mom, *Lucy Lee*; for being my fresh eyes, I am so glad God chose her to be a part of this assignment.

Thank you to each and every one of you. I Love you with my whole heart...

About the Author

Elana L. Burnes is a 55 your old Master Cosmetologist that resides in Miami Florida. She has had experiences that has led her to her current calling in ministry. Becoming a teenage mother at the age of 17, led her to have the strength and endurance to persevere.

She has also taken courses to become a substance abuse counselor, while pursuing her career in cosmetology. Yet her true calling and passion and ultimate goal was to become a certified life coach. However; as soon as she neared the end of the course God revealed to her that she was called to the ministry. At last she is fulfilling her ultimate desire to coach, she is just now coaching and leading others through the word of Jesus Christ.

Message from Author

I am grateful. There is nothing greater than, hearing the Lord's voice, being obedient, and walking in your God given purpose. I now know the reason for my birth. I am fulfilled. I am so glad that God saw fit for me to be the person I am today. From the major loses I have experienced, to taking control of my own life, and ultimately, living for God, and loving Him with my whole heart. I totally know from where my help comes from… My God!!!

THE GIFT BIRTHED…AFTER MY LOSS

INTRODUCTION

As the Holy Spirit awakens me in the morning I meditate. As I meditate He places a word in my spirit. The words that God have been giving me for passages every morning, are words that range from Press to Swish Swash, I would have days where I would ask the Lord what in the world am I supposed to do with that word. Well sure enough, an inspirational passage would soon be developed after that. I have been walking in this assignment for nearly two years now. I realize He gave me a platform and this is now a part of my ministry. I have been faithful to this assignment I do not miss a morning. He is using me to encourage people every day. At this point I have written well over five hundred passages.

In the beginning I didn't understand the gift but as time went on, I realized that this is God's unique way of making me study I have had to define words, then look to see how they are used in sentences. I would then seek to find scriptures that are connected to the word, a little while after I had been writing God revealed to me that He was calling me to the ministry; so, writing wasn't just about passages, He was training me and giving me a system to go by. Now, along with any word that He places in my spirit, He also leads me to create a passage. This has been a true boot camp experience, at its finest. I have had to write at all times of the morning. These passages are meant to help and motivate God's people as they experience the trials of everyday life.

As you read each inspirational passage there is a picture attached to the passage. What I have also learned was to recognize the beauty of God's creations in the world around me. As I am out, and about certain things catch my eye. I have learned to appreciate the beauty of nature. The pictures may not necessarily correspond with what the words of the passage are reflecting; however, what I have learned is no matter what situation you are facing there is always something beautiful in the world that surrounds us. All we have to do is take the time to meditate, reflect and allow our natural surroundings to be a natural psychotic drug that will make us appreciate where we are no matter the situation. I challenge you to find beauty in the world that surrounds you and capture it.

It Is Real!

Yet!
You still live!
Don't suppress what you feel!
Process whatever it is!
So you're able to cope with the ordeal!
You are stronger than you know!
And don't feel like you're in it alone!
You can do it!
Push through!
Somebody needs you!
Your praise report!
Is gonna help someone else!
Stand up straight!
There's no need to be a afraid!
You were created to be!
Tough and brave!
Continue to hang in there!
And keep the Faith!

Love and Hugs!
(Psalm 18:2)
God is your strength and your rock!

Practice Makes Perfect!

Keep working!
The Blessings you have coming!
You are deserving!
You may not see it now!
But keep going and doing!
God sees your good works!
Nothing is in vain!
Sometimes there may be some pain!
But He uses it all!
And turns it around!
And makes it work out for your good!
Do it with Love!
And stay focused!
Your season of Blessings!
Will be here!
Before you know it!

Love and Hugs!
God hasn't forgotten you!
Blessings!

Pick Up the Pieces!

It's not always easy!
When you just don't see no way!
Call on the name of Jesus!
He's right there!
To help you!
With those things!
That are just so hard to bear!
Life doesn't always feel like it's fair!
But He can!
Bring you back together!
He can keep you In the worst!
Types of weather!
Hold on!
It's going to get better!
It's okay to get weary and tired!
But trust and believe!
You can!
Get to the other side!

Love and Hugs!
Jesus never leaves!
Blessings!
(Pic by Barbara Thomas)

Don't Give into The Pressure!

Have some restraint!
You have the power!
Things can go from zero to sixty!
In just one hour!
Life can be sweet one minute!
And then turn completely sour!
But you can stand through it all!
Always remember!
To put on the full armor of God!
Fill up with the word!
So, when something comes up!
You won't be disturbed!
Protect your joy and your peace!
You need it intact!
So, you can walk through a storm!
And come out!
On your feet!

Love and Hugs!
Put on the full armor of God!
(Ephesians 6: 11-18)
Blessings!

Great Minds!

Learn to slow down!
And make sure you're doing fine!
Don't keep your brain on overload all the time!
Bring it down just a notch!
It's very easy to do too much!
Find a good balance!
So, you'll have the endurance to last!
No one ever said you had to go through your
Journey really fast!
You don't want to get ahead of God!
You need to stay in alignment with Him!
He orders your steps!
You didn't design your path yourself!
He's your guide!
And your help!
Walking with Him!
Helps you see things!
As they develop!

Love and Hugs!
Stay with God!
And take good care of your mind body and soul!
Blessings!

Share Some Love!

It's doesn't take much!
And it doesn't cost a thing!
But you never know!
How much joy it brings!
Just a kind word!
Does wonders!
When People's spirits are low!
A smile and simple hello!
Makes a difference!
Kind gestures go very far!
You don't know who's!
Walking around!
With a broken heart!
You can't always see pain from the outside!
Go that extra mile to be nice!
Find ways to brighten!
Someone's life!

Love and Hugs!
God is Love!
You can't Love God and not Love people!
Blessings!

Piece It Together!

Piece by piece!
Day by day!
And take one step at a time!
That's the way God works with you!
He gives a little here and a little there!
He can't give you everything at once!
You would not be able to handle it!
He has to teach you patience during your race!
And take you at a nice pace!
Along the way you have to get the lesson!
And He has to give wisdom and understanding!
You won't ever be able to rush God!
Keep that on your heart!
Just let Him lead!
And you do your part!

Love and Hugs!
God knows how to process you!
He is in control!
Blessings!

It's A Brand-New Day!

Continue to celebrate!
If it's only because you're awake!
That's the most important reason!
Enjoying family and good eating!
Those are major blessings!
Don't take them for granted!
There are people in places!
That are numb and alone!
All they can feel is their heart aching!
No matter where you are!
At this very moment!
Trust and believe!
It's better than!
Where you could be!
Be happy and pleased!
There's someone somewhere!
That would love!
To take your seat!

Love and Hugs!
Thank God for all He has done
He didn't have to do it!
Blessings!

Dare to Begin!

Even when there's heaviness within!
Just do the best you can!
There isn't anything written in stone!
Saying how you should be moving along!
It's your Journey and yours alone!
Everyone processes things differently!
The trials of life take everyone on different routes!
No one can tell you how to drive in your lane!
Or what speed you should be driving at!
That is totally up to you!
And you don't have to explain!
Only God and you!
Know!
How you're able!
To dance in the rain!
He helps with the heavy strain!
That's the only way!
You can go that extra mile!
With a smile!

Love and Hugs
Thank God for it all!
Blessings!

In Order to Scratch the Surface!

On what God can do with you!
If you're a believer!
Obedience is the key!
Obedience opens doors!
Obedience takes you to powerful places you
would never have experienced!
Use what you have been given!
Complete your assignments!
If you don't understand!
Continue doing it anyway!
A lot of the time it won't even make sense!
That's just the way God does business!
There's a purpose for everything He gives you!
That's why the scripture says!
Trust in the Lord with all thine heart; and lean not
unto thine own understanding! **(Pro 3:5)**
Keep going and trusting He's got you in His
hands!
Don't worry and don't be in a hurry!
When He's ready!
He will show you a part of the plan!

Love and Hugs!
Keep Trusting and keep moving!
Blessings!

There's a Special Delivery!

That's just for you!
God sends His love!
From above!
There's a peace that surpasses all understanding!
And it's available to you!
Doesn't matter what you've gone through!
He can make it better!
Only He!
Can give you a peace that brings you to tears!
And give you the courage!
To walk past all your fears!
He knows about all the pain you feel!
He's a Master!
At helping you heal!
Give it all to Him!
He's there for you!
In the midst!
Of whatever!
You're dealing with!

Love and Hugs!
Lean on God with all you have in you!
Blessings!

Whip!

Get up!
Get going!
And walk boldly in your Gift!
The one called life!
No matter what tries to hold you back!
Keep telling yourself it's going to be alright!
You were already equipped for the fight!
As you go through your day!
Repeat to yourself!
I can do all things through Christ! **(Phil 4:13)**
Who strengthens me!
Speak it!
And get it deep down in your being!
That will be!
Just the beginning!
When you can stand on God's word!
You are winning!
You are ready for the world!

Love and Hugs!
Stand firmly on the word of God!
Blessings!

Sweep!

Keep things nice and neat!
Thank God for shelter!
And the blessing of having food to eat!
You are blessed beyond measure!
You don't have to roll up a blanket!
And find a place to sleep on the street!
You have both feet!
You are doing well!
Even though the hills you have to climb!
They may tend to feel a little steep!
But Thank God, He doesn't miss a beat!
He's right there in the midst!
He always gives you the push that you need!
When you feel like you have lost your way!
Don't worry!
Just keep praying!
And being patient!
God just may be sending you!
In a different direction!

Love and Hugs!
God never leaves your side!
Count your blessings!

Get Grounded!

If you would please!
You can call on the name of Jesus!
With ease!
Yes indeed!
He's the reason you can be set free!
He heals diseases!
He will supply all of your needs!
He's with you through thick and thin!
He will forgive you of your sins!
It is the greatest feeling in the world!
Just to know Him!
When you give Him your hand!
It gets easier to stand!
He's the only one!
Who can take your pain!
And do a brand-new thing!
The joy you get in your heart!
Will definitely!
Make you sing!

Love and Hugs!
Thank Jesus for all He has done! Blessings!

It's Easy for Things to Get Twisted!

Ask God to help you with it!
Life can change at the flick of a wrist!
Do your best to hang in there!
When life starts to shift!
The Holidays are fast approaching!
Everyone isn't making a list!
This is the time of year!
When!
People that have experienced a loss!
Have their hardest moments!
Be sensitive to their needs!
Let them know you care!
Allow them to do what they feel!
They just may not want to be!
Out and about everywhere!
Try and understand tradition for them!
Has changed!
It's a lot different!
And it's okay if they just want to do!
Something simple!

Love and Hugs!
God will bring you through! Blessings!

A Little Spat!

Can turn into something huge!
If you don't diffuse it right away!
Make peace quickly!
Do your best not carry little things on and on!
Until it starts to take you out of your zone!
It doesn't take much to throw you off course!
Stay focused!
Live with peace in your heart!
Life can already get hard!
You don't need the extra!
Keep your life light!
Be flexible!
Try not to run on such a tight schedule!
Take time to just breathe!
Seize precious moments!
Enjoy the awesome blessing!
Of just being able!
To feel a nice breeze!

Love and Hugs!
Fight for Your Peace!
And stay with God!
Blessings!

Paste!

At times life can!
Tend to leave you with a bitter taste!
But at the end of the day!
You still have to keep moving!
You can't get from first base to second!
By standing in place!
You have to keep running!
You can't give up part of the way there!
That's how life is!
You can't quit!
Throwing in the towel is not an option!
You have come too far!
When you feel like you are about to break!
That means you're breaking through!
You can't be molded!
If you haven't been broken!
You have to go through!
To get to!
The new you!

Love and Hugs!
Allow God to build you up! Blessings!

God Is Always Available!

You can meet Him anywhere!
He's in your living room!
While you're sitting in your chair!
He listens to all!
You would like to share!
And when you talk with Him!
There's one thing about it!
It's not going anywhere!
He's the wind!
He's the fresh air!
He's just and He is fair!
He's the one!
You can count on!
When no one else is there!
Trust and believe!
He loves you!
And He cares!

Love and Hugs!
God will never leave nor forsake you! Blessings!

Aim to Please!

Put your best foot forward in all things!
Whatever you put your mind to!
Give it your all!
If you half, do!
It may just come back on you!
It's just like your reputation!
Your character speaks for itself!
Live your best life!
Being your best self!
So, when your name is ringing in the street!
The battle is already won!
Because deep down in your being you know how you've
been   living!
So, while people are talking!
You keep walking!
It's a distraction!
And waisted energy anyway!
Don't allow it to take you!
Out of the race!
Keep moving!
With grace!
 Love and Hugs! Give God your best!

There's No Need for Greed!

It destroys!
It causes you to do the wrong things!
For the wrong reasons!
If you totally Trust and believe in the Lord!
He will supply all of your needs!
And anything else He wants to bless you with!
Comes in due season!
When you get anything the wrong way!
It will never pay!
You won't have any peace about it!
And takes your life down the wrong path!
And it doesn't last!
It's not hard to do what's right!
Be patient!
And wait on your blessings!
So you can sleep at night!
Love and Hugs!
Wait on God He's always on time!
Blessings!

Fill in the Blank!

Any way you like!
It is your life!
As long as you're fulfilled!
Don't rely on anyone else!
To give you what you're missing!
People places or things!
Will not complete you!
Be at peace right where you are!
And create the happiness!
That you're looking for!
Life should never feel boring!
You have too much going!
Love you!
With your whole heart!
And don't allow anyone!
To come along!
And tear it apart!

Love and Hugs!
When you Have God you have it all!

Relax the Mind!

Look at the bright side!
Of all the things that matter!
Try to find something positive in every
situation!
It may not be easy!
Just keep in mind!
It could always be worse!
Then things may be a little easier to handle!
No one ever said life would be a piece of cake!
But you decide what you bake!
You can share beautiful slices!
Or you can send out the pieces that are burnt on
all sides!
Whatever you put out!
That's what will be coming back!
Try your best to do what's right!
Live a loving!
And joyous life!

Love and Hugs!
God is always on your side!
Blessings!

Go Ahead and Cry!

Crying doesn't always mean sadness!
When the heart is happy!
The tears will over flow!
When you have so much joy on the inside!
Just let it go!
It's okay!
It's good for the soul!
It doesn't mean you're not strong!
Your heart is just beating!
To a beautiful song!
A good release!
Is always needed!
And when the joy of the Lord is upon you!
It gets deep!
You are going to weep!
It is the most amazing feeling!
When the soul gets what it needs!

Love and Hugs!
(John 11:35)
Jesus wept.
Blessings!

Begin Again!

A bad season is not the end!
You have what it takes!
God knows!
What will help you grow in a certain area!
To be credible in anything!
You have to have firsthand experience!
You don't know what He's building in you!
So keep pushing through!
He has to prepare you before He takes you anywhere!
So appreciate every step you make!
Big or small!
Progress is progress!
As long as you're moving forward!
The Journey doesn't end because you may be
low or weary!
Nope!
God gives you a second wind!
He is the strength beneath!
Your wings!

Love and Hugs!
(Proverbs 3:5)
Trust the Lord with all thine heart: and lean not onto thy own
understanding.

Grin and Bear It!

There's so much hurt and pain everywhere!
Every day there's another heart!
With a great big tear!
Continue sending out your prayers!
Lift as many people as you can!
Show some Love and kindness!
People carry some heavy loads!
You never know what cause them to explode!
Sometimes it takes everything in them!
Just to drive a mile down the road!
People battle things you never know about!
Try your best to be a light!
It doesn't take much for someone's life!
To take a different route!
At the blink of an eye!
Things could feel so bad!
Before you know it!
You are so overwhelmed!
You feel like!
You just can't fight!
Love and Hugs!
(Psalm 61:2)
From the end of the earth will I cry unto thee, when my heart is overwhelmed: lead me to the rock that is higher than

Enjoy Your Journey!

You have to go through some things!
It's designed to build you up!
Not to bring you down!
Keep holding on!
You're going to get stronger! ♥ 😘

Press On!

Go forward!
Nervousness is normal!
Keep stepping!
God wants to take you somewhere!
It's okay to feel like!
You're about to come unglued!
It's only because you are about to walk into something new!
You have no reason to be afraid!
You can do it!
Those sounds of fear that you hear!
Are overrated!
Once you start diffusing the doubt!
And walking past the fear!
You won't even remember it was there!
You were prepared for where you're going!
A long time ago!
You just didn't know!

Love and Hugs!
(Psalm 32:8)
I will instruct thee and teach thee in the way which though shalt go: I will guide thee with mine eye.

Be True to You!

In All That You Do!
Your story is for God's Glory!
He brought you through!
For someone else to pull from you!
To give them some hope!
Because when they see!
How He did it for you they are able to fight a little bit
harder!
Knowing He can do it for them!
God doesn't just show His power for no reason!
You are somebody's life jacket!
People are drowning!
Don't take it lightly!
You be the reason!
Someone else!
Keeps fighting!

Love and Hugs!
Allow God to use your pain to bring someone else out of
the rain!
Blessings!

Pick and Choose!

What would you like to do!
You want to win or lose!
You want to walk in your shoes!
Or blend with others!
Would you wear bright colors!
Or you rather the dull ones!
Could you walk alone!
If God needed you to!
In order to take you to a whole 'nother realm!
If so, If you're truly willing!
Just say Lord here I am!
You can't go where He wants to take you!
And continue doing things the same!
If you're going to walk with God!
There will be some changes!
You have to be willing to step out of the box!
And leave some stuff behind!
No worries you will be just fine!
He's the only one!
Who can lead you!
To the mountain top!

Love and Hugs!
(Ephesians 2:10)
For we are his workmanship, created in Christ Jesus unto good works, which
God hath ordained that we should walk in Him.

Insecurities!

Can paralyze you!
Don't give into them!
Press through!
God designed an Amazing path for you!
Don't allow anything to cloud your mind!
Any feelings or thoughts that come up!
That are not pushing you forward!
Block them out!
You don't want to fall behind!
Bind anything that doesn't make you feel good about you!
You don't lack anything!
You are a powerful being!
Created with all that you need!
Don't allow the trick of the enemy!
To get in your spirit!
And plant seeds!
That make you feel defeated!

Love and Hugs!
(Psalm 139:14)
I will Praise thee; for I am fearfully and wonderfully made: marvelous are thy works; and that my soul knoweth right well.

Once You Have Been Set Free!

From whatever!
Has held you down!
Don't go back into bondage!
You can't afford to allow the old baggage to creep back in!
You can't be who you're intended to be!
If you're bogged down with heaviness on the inside!
You can't rise!
With your wings tied!
You were created!
To soar up high!
But your spirit!
Has to be light!
Before!
You can take flight!
Be bold enough!
To take control of your life!

Love and Hugs!
(John 8:36)
If the Son therefore shall make you free, ye shall be free indeed.

Freeze!

Be still!
And listen to God!
If you will!
Having some type of direction!
Is a really big deal!
Anything you want to know!
He will show you!
But you have to be in tune!
You have to have a relationship!
And the more it develops!
The brighter your life gets!
The darkness!
Starts to turn to light!
Your battles!
You no longer have to fight!
Being in Christ!
Is when life!
Truly begins!
There's a peace!
And an unexplainable joy!
That never ends!

(John 8:12)
Then spake Jesus again unto them, saying, I am the light of the world: he that followeth me shall not walk in darkness, but shall have the light of life.

Scream!

Don't hold things in!
Until you feel like!
You're about to bust loose at the seams!
Release the steam!
Free yourself!
So, you can focus on other things!
You have bigger fish to fry!
You have visions and dreams!
All bottled up inside!
There are so many things you have never tried!
There's a life waiting on you!
That is yet to be seen!
You just have to decide!
When you're going to take that leap of faith!
And experience!
All of your greatness!

Love and Hugs!
Walking with God you can do it all!

Don't Bite Off More Than You Can Chew!

It's not good for you!
If you're all over the place!
Your immune system will pay!
Without balance!
There's no way you can do well!
In every area!
Find a way to narrow some things down!
Don't continue running around and around!
Because you will find yourself!
Feeling like you're going to drown!
Pace yourself!
Know what's best!
So, you can continue on!
God needs you!
To finish strong!

Love and Hugs!
You have to take good care of you!
          Let the spirit of God lead you!

Make Your Bed!

Make sure your spirit is fed!
Everyday!
Life can tend to feel a little gray!
At times!
But the word of God!
Makes you come alive!
On the inside!
You will have bad days!
There will be days when you're just sad!
But make the best of your day anyway!
Speak a word of gratitude!
It helps when you're going through!
If you can dress up!
And put on some shoes!
You're doing pretty good!
Enjoy what you can!
Being of sound mind!
Is wealth!
Enjoy your riches!
While you're living!

Love and Hugs!
                    Praise God from whom all blessings flow!

Resist Bad Connections!

You don't want to continue!
To be someone's lesson!
Don't fall for the wrong type of affection!
Know who you are!
You are definitely!
Somebody's blessing!
Focus on being whole!
When God designed you!
He broke the mold!
You don't need anyone to validate you!
Don't ever lose you!
Putting so much into someone else!
You are priority!
Make sure you are happy within!
So, when God sends someone!
It will be a perfect blend!

Love and Hugs!
Wait on God!
Blessings!

Push Through the Pain!

One day you'll wake up!
And you won't feel as drained!
Grief takes you to a place!
You cannot explain!
You will have days when you're just walking along!
Functioning okay!
And out of nowhere tears!
Just start over flowing!
It's like the flood gates have opened up!
Have your moment!
Grief doesn't just go away!
Deal with it your way!
You can't rush the process!
Keep praying!
And be sure to get your rest!
Loss takes a toll on you!
It's takes some time to get your strength back!
Take your time!
Do the best you can!
God has you!
In the palm of His hand!

Love and Hugs!
        Father God lift and comfort every heavy heart!

Build Your Bridges on High!

Don't ever stop!
Reaching for the sky!
You may get tired!
But don't lose!
The burning desire!
To live at your best!
Take in what you need!
And leave the rest!
Keep heading in the right direction!
And on God's time!
He makes all those pieces of your journey!
That you have received!
It all comes together!
And makes the most!
Rewarding connection!
So, don't work so hard!
Trying to figure it all out!
Just keep Trusting God!

Love and Hugs!
God is leading the way!
You just don't realize it! Blessings!

Seek to Have Peace!

The more peaceful!
You are!
The more you can hear God speak!
Find quiet places!
That are calming!
Where your mind won't be racing!
To get what you need!
You have to find time!
To stretch and reach!
Out to God!
It's not hard!
But you have to be willing!
God is always around!
You just have to decide!
To give Him some time!
Allow God in your heart!
He can help you!
Because life!
Truly does get hard!

Love and Hugs!
God is bigger than any situation! Blessings!

Take It All In!

As your day begins!
Thank God!
Your lungs are clear!
Breathe in and out!
Now you have thee!
Most important reason to shout!
As you go out and about!
Walk in boldness today!
And leave the doubt!
You can handle whatever comes into play!
Don't take in anything!
That doesn't brighten your space!
If you feel any negative spirits!
Coming close!
Start to pray within!
Smile!
And begin to walk the other way!
Humming!
And continuing to!
Claim your day!

Love and Hugs! God gives you the strength to endure! Blessings!

When There's a Bruise!

Keep getting up!
And putting on your shoes!
You can still be used!
By God!
Not by people!
When it gets hard!
God stays by your side!
He can't run and hide!
And if you fall!
He will!
Pick you up!
Turn you around!
And plant your feet!
On solid ground!
You can depend on Him!
He will never leave you!
Hanging out!
On a limb!
Love and Hugs! You can't do anything without God! Blessings!

Replace!

Whatever left you with a bad taste!
Turn it into something with a sweet base!
And continue on your way!
In life you always have to take!
The bitter with sweet!
Just don't let it knock you off your feet!
You have places to go!
And people to meet!
You have been given Grace!
You can't easily be defeated!
Carry on!
Continue to be strong!
Remember!
You don't do anything alone!
God is there!
When you feel despair trying to show up!
Send that spirit!
Somewhere else!
And rest in the Almighty!
Who definitely cares!

Love and Hugs! Stand on your Faith! God is with you during your race!

Step!

Your day has already been set!
Make the best of it!
Make it great!
Block out anything!
That's aggravating!
Claim peace throughout your day!
Refuse!
To allow it to go any other way!
You determine what you want!
You set the stage!
You direct the play!
You have the power!
You can have peace and joy!
Or you can just allow things!
To keep you annoyed!
Your days are precious!
Treat each and every one!
As a wonderful blessing!

Love and Hugs! True peace and love is of God! Blessings!

Regroup!

Don't just sit on the stoop!
Rise up!
Above everything!
That was meant to hurt you!
Let go of the old!
So, you can receive the new!
Don't let anything hold you down!
You keep going!
You are strong enough!
You are worthy!
God had a Great plan for you!
Before your birth!
You have a unique purpose!
Walk in it!
With your head up!
And your shoulders back!
Drop off anything!
That you have to drag!

Love and Hugs!
God knows the plan He has for you!
Trust it! Blessings!

It's Good to Reflect on Your Past!

It reminds you that!
Those storms you were in!
Didn't last!
You made it through before!
And you will make it through again!
You put up a good fight!
And you held on till the bitter end!
As long as you're breathing!
You will have to go through something!
At some point!
Life is just full of different seasons!
Everyone has to have theirs!
For different reasons!
There's no way around it!
But don't lose hope!
Just know!
That during every rough patch!
God has your back!

Love and Hugs!
The storms of life will come and go!
But God is always with you! Blessings!

Let God Be God!

You keep praying!
And doing your part!
Whatever you're praying for!
It's not too hard!
For Him!
He's the only one!
That can clean up the heart!
He's the only one that cause a change in people!
You pray and wait!
And let God!
Have His way!
He knows how to do what you need!
You can't tell Him how to do it!
Or when!
Just give it to Him!
And be patient!
And remember!
God is never late!

Love and Hugs! There is nothing too hard for God! Blessings!

Be Comfortable!

Every day won't always feel wonderful!
But remain humble!
You have so many reasons to be Thankful!
Do your very best not to complain!
God does not like complaining or grumbling!
It's bad on your life!
Even when you're going through!
Think about it!
God has still been good to you!
You have all that you need!
Your eyes are open!
And you're breathing!
Sometime ago!
You probably didn't even think!
You would walk into a new season!
He is continually blessing!
Don't forget to Thank Him!
He didn't have to do it!
But He did!
　　　Love and Hugs! God will supply all your needs! Blessings!

Run!

You have to continue!
Until your time here is done!
It won't always be fun!
But God has entrusted you with something!
Don't take it lightly!
Do it with joy in your heart!
Take pride in whatever it is!
When you use what you have been given!
The more He will give!
Love it and live it!
Whatever He has bestowed upon you!
It is an Honor!
Let Him know you are grateful!
Because it can always be taken away!
God Has blessed you with something special!
Don't keep it buried!
Decide to do something with it!
And don't worry!
You will do well!

God equips you for whatever He gives you!
Don't allow fear to hold you back! Blessings

Rewind!

Take a look around!
You're gonna be just fine!
God has brought you through before!
And He will do it again this time!
Just don't give up!
He knows when you have had enough!
Your job is to continue to Trust!
Your breakthrough is coming!
Focus on staying strong!
Because you!
Are gonna need some energy for where you're going!
He's been working behind the scene all along!
You just didn't know!
So keep you together!
So, when it's time!
You will be ready to go!

Love and Hugs!
Hang in there!
God knows what He's doing!
Blessings!

Having Peace Within!

There's peace of mind!
And there's peace and quiet!
But then there's a peace!
That only God can give!
It's a peace that never leaves!
A peace you can't explain!
It truly does surpass all understanding!
No matter what's happening in the world!
You have peace!
When you have received it!
It's a different feeling!
Everything can get crazy!
But you still have peace and joy!
So instead of getting all out of sorts!
You Praise and sing!
It is the most!
Beautiful thing!

Love and Hugs!
(John 14:27)
Peace I leave with you, My peace I give unto you: not as the
world giveth, give I unto you. Let not Your heart be troubled, neither
let it be afraid

Master Your Craft!

Be diligent!
You were handpicked!
For that certain gift and skill!
Once it has been revealed!
Do your very best with it!
Whatever you don't use!
You can lose!
If God gives you something to do!
And you don't move on it!
He will choose someone else!
Don't lose your God given vision or gift!
That would truly be heart breaking!
Once you receive it!
Go with it!
When God wants you to move on something!
You don't have anything to lose!
He prepared you a long time ago!
To be used!

Love and Hugs!
Trust God all the way through the process!

In Place!

Because of God's Amazing Grace!
Lord you are worthy of every Praise!
Every day!
In every way!
This isn't just a regular day by any means!
There were so many things heard!
But not seen!
The winds were high!
And sounded like loud screaming!
The sky's roared!
There were so many reasons to worry!
But you Lord!
You kept us safe!
You brought us through!
And gave us a brand-new story!
We Praise your mighty name!
And give you all the Glory!

Love and Hugs!
Lord Thank you for Bringing us through the storm!
Blessings!

Hold on To Your Faith!

God is the Greatest!
If you're anchored in Him!
You're in a good place!
He Truly is peace in the midst!
He controls everything!
Even this!
He's the only one!
That can give you the most precious gift!
He touches you every morning!
And causes your eyelids to lift!
He can cause a major shift!
Nice and swift!
There's nothing else better!
Than Knowing Him!
Keep Trusting!
And looking up!
To the hills!

Love and Hugs!
Praise God in the midst of your storm! Blessings!

Shower!

Each other with love!
Like the all Mighty does!
He doesn't pick and choose!
He loves everyone!
And that's what we are here to do!
To love and help each other!
And lend a hand!
To any of our Brothers or Sisters!
Do what you can!
Put all your fears in God's hands!
And know!
He is your strength!
In the midst of any storm!
Find peace in Him!
Because He!
Can make anything stand still!

Love and Hugs!
God is!!! Blessings!

Present Your Best Self!

At all times!
Don't allow others to bring out the worst in you!
If someone wants to act up!
Put a smile on your face!
Handle it in a nice way!
And walk away with Grace!
It won't always be easy!
But try to do the best that you can!
Some things are sent to test you!
You don't want to keep failing!
God can't take you any further!
Until you get past some things!
He has to mature you!
Before He gets you to a place!
Where you are ready!
To spread your wings!
Press forward!
And get ready to do!
Some new things!
Love and Hugs!
Let's continue to pray for each other! Blessings!

Sweat!

Don't let folks see you sweat!
Be strong be courageous!
Do your best!
Don't sweat the small stuff!
Life is already hard enough!
Keep your mind on God!
You know He has been there from the start!
He's there when the seas are calm!
When the storms are roaring!
When the hard winds are blowing!
Even when the sun is beautiful and glowing!
He's in Control of it all!
Things can get a little crazy!
But keep holding on!
And Trusting!
And know!
That through it all!
God is still Amazing!

Love and Hugs!
Hold on God is with you! Blessings!

Branches!

Step out and take chances!
You get a new day!
To embrace change!
Every day is never the same!
Don't be afraid to try a new thing!
If it's in your spirit!
You should try it!
You never know what it will lead you to!
When something stirs up on the inside!
Most of the time there's a good reason why!
You have gifts inside that have never been tapped into!
You don't know what you can do!
If you don't want to experience anything new!
Don't ever stop trying and doing!
You don't know!
What all God has planted inside of you!

Love and Hugs!
Use what God has given you!
Blessings!

Under Your Belt!

You have experiences galore!
Some came easy!
Where others may have caused you to want to lay out across the floor!
You have days where you have wept!
But you continued on!
And took that next step!
All experiences are not good!
But it serves a purpose!
Once you have gone through something first hand!
It gives you credibility!
Every experience!
Will help you!
To fulfill your destiny!

Love and Hugs!
Trust God's plan!
Blessings!

Dip in And Seek!

Get in the word!
All week!
Listen!
When God speaks!
Feed your spirit!
Before anything else gets in!
You have to be built up!
In order to stay strong!
You never know what may come along!
Always put your armor on!
Protect you!
Sometimes things happen just to test you!
Keep you at your best!
So you can avoid some stress!
And all things that are unnecessary!

Love and Hugs!
Father God watch over our children!
Blessings!

Be Quick to Forgive!

It keeps you light!
It helps you heal!
It takes the pressure off your heart!
Unforgiveness!
Robs and steals!
It takes your joy!
It can cause brokenness and bitterness!
Take it to God!
He wants you to be happy and whole!
Allow him to work!
Deep down in your soul!
He wants you to shine!
Like pure Gold!
You are not here to live!
Bitter and torn!

Love and Hugs!
There isn't anything too big for God! Blessings

When Your Name Is Dragged!

Through the mud!
Keep smiling and showing Love!
And giving Hugs!
Your reputation speaks for itself!
From time to time!
Things may go left!
Let it roll off your back!
You have to be able to rise above!
All of that!
Especially if you're expecting next level!
You have to be able to hold it together!
You can't be blown over!
Every time a hard wind comes through!
You have to stand!
Stay focused!
And allow God to guide you!
To where he needs you to be!

Love and Hugs! Let God fight your battles! Blessings!

Breathe In!

Breathe Out!
Live out loud!
You're still here to Live and Love!
That's what's it's all about!
Be proud!
Of who you are!
You had to go over some hills!
And through some valleys!
You may even have a few scars!
But you are better for it!
You are Amazing!
Keep Praising!
There's no reason to walk!
In anyone else's shadow!
The All Mighty!
Is the only one!
You should want to follow!

Love and Hugs God is Love! You should Love! Blessings!

Coat Your Stomach!

Before taking most medicines!
Guard your heart!
At all times!
Cover your entire being!
With the word of God!
It's never too late to start!
This world is cruel!
And hard!
But God created born fighters!
Believing and trusting in Him!
Makes all the difference!
He makes your burdens lighter!
He lightens your load!
He walks with you!
When you feel like you're!
Going down a long dreary road!
No worries!
You are never on your own!

Love and Hugs!
Trust and walk with God! Blessings!

Turn Up the Music!

Pat your feet!
And enjoy the beat!
Live and enjoy!
You may feel a little depleted!
At times!
But lean on your Faith!
You cannot be defeated!
You may be going through the fire!
But you are equipped to withstand heat!
Keep going!
And letting God lead!
He's knows where he wants you to go!
He knows what you need!
Trust him!
Be a good tree!
And plant the best seeds!

Love and Hugs! God is always with you! Blessings!

Take Time to Enjoy the Sky!

And think about how God!
Always supplies!
You may feel like you don't have as much as you want!
But your needs are met!
If you have Shelter, food lights and water!
You're doing good!
You are blessed with a job!
You have clothing!
Whatever you are in need of!
He supplies!
When your Spirit is low!
He sends a word to lift you!
When you get too deep down in the Valley!
He sends someone to pull you out!
Things don't happen by chance!
God is working!
In the midst of things you may not understand!
But just know!
You're in good hands!

Love and Hugs!
                    God will take care of you! Blessings!

Force Your Way Through the Day!

Something will always try to get in your way!
Talk yourself through it!
Claim the type of day you want to have!
Receive it!
And take control of the energy you would like!
Some days you just don't feel right!
But make the best of It!
Put your best foot forward!
Take your mind to beautiful place!
Get gratefulness in your spirit!
And think of all those reasons you have to smile inside!
Being alive!
Is a good enough reason to have an awesome day!
Listen to positive thoughts!
Instead of negative talk!
Be careful of what you except in your space!
That's the best way to keep a smile on your face!

Love and Hugs!
Praise God for every day you get!
Blessings!

Try to Live Without Regret!

When you want to try something new!
Change your mind set!
The sky is the limit!
The more you start to get pass those things that you are afraid of!
The better it gets!
When you conquer fear!
It's a really big deal!
Not being able to go forward!
Can cause you to get depressed!
And keep you down!
God didn't create you to be bound!
You have the ability to do those things you set your mind to do!
It's up to you!
Plant Powerful words on the inside!
Once you get a burning desire!
It's sparks a fire!
Then it takes you higher!

Love and Hugs!
Trust God and take a step!
Blessings!

ELANA BURNES

Lift and Not Blame!

Every day will not be the same!
Count it a blessing!
Whether it's sunny or raining!
Yes!
The storms you go through can be draining!
But keep going and Praising!
Take each day as it comes!
Celebrate!
You're getting a full meal!
Some may only have crumbs!
There is so much to be Thankful for!
Even after you have been shaken to the core!
If you can get up and walk across the floor!
Thank God!
You are blessed beyond measure!
Life is Precious!
You are a Golden treasure!

Love and Hugs! Thank God for all he has done! Blessings!

Made in the USA
Columbia, SC
14 February 2018